SILENCE AND OTHER SURPRISING INVITATIONS OF ADVENT

Enuma Okoro

UPPER
ROOM BOOKS®
NASHVILLE

For Lisa Yebuah,
who has expanded my
holy imagination

CONTENTS

PART 1: SURPRISED AND SILENCED BY GOD

Week One: Zechariah

Week Two: Elizabeth & Zechariah

PART 2: PREPARATION AND LABORING WITH GOD'S PROMISES

Week Three: Elizabeth, Mary, & John

PART 3: TRUSTING AND RECEIVING GOD'S WORD

Week Four: The Community Trusts the Word

Preface

Advent is the first season in the Christian liturgical calendar. Derived from the Latin word *adventus* and the Greek word *parousia*, it means "coming" and refers to the coming of Christ. Christians recognize the four weeks of Advent as a time to anticipate the birth of the Christ child and the second coming of Christ at final judgment. During Advent we repent of the habits and practices that turn us away from the loving God who is always reaching out to be reconciled to us. We want to become a people who seek after God and who cultivate patience as we wait for divine justice to bring peace and freedom to an aching world. As we reflect on the Advent scripture narrative, we are invited to walk alongside faithful men and women who also sought after God and waited upon God to answer their prayers and to keep God's promises of salvation and freedom from injustice and oppression. We walk alongside men and women like Zechariah, Elizabeth, and Mary who were familiar with intimate encounters with God that startled them into silence, awed them into seclusion, and inspired them to praise and thanksgiving.

Most Advent reflections center on the Annunciation, the angel Gabriel's visitation to Mary to pronounce God's favor upon her and her role as Theotokos, the Christ-bearer. This book shifts the Advent attention to Zechariah and Elizabeth, the two elderly, devout Jews who miraculously conceived John the Baptist. Theirs is a story of accustomed longing and unmet desire, sustained prayer, occasional doubt, and seasons of silent retreat and seclusion. We can learn much about the tensions of a genuine faith journey from the trials and surprises that Zechariah and Elizabeth encountered in their attempts to live before God. And we can learn about the mercy and faithfulness of a God who acts in God's own timing and for God's wider purposes.

Like those who witnessed the first coming of Christ, we hear God beckon us during Advent to make ourselves available to God in new and courageous ways. We are invited to practice a unique kind of hospitality with one another: the sort of hospitality that makes room for people to share the strange ways in which God is moving in their lives; the sort of hospitality that encourages people to put down wearisome baggage and trust God to fill their empty hands and hearts; the sort of hospitality that nurtures space for holy listening. This hospitality encourages others to believe that God is always in the business of making things new, bringing life into spaces that feel barren, and strengthening the weak to receive and offer the gifts of God.

Advent is a season to ponder, to listen, to understand that prayer is as much about cultivating stillness and attentiveness as it is about offering our words to God. This listening for God is a difficult business. It requires a willingness to be patient and to be still. It requires disciplining ourselves to consistent times of sitting quietly before God and waiting for God to meet us in that space. When we are still we can better attune ourselves to the thoughts and feelings that well up within. Contemplative prayer, the posture of listening for God in silence, is a distinct type of praying that opens our entire selves up to hear and receive God in possibly surprising ways. It requires a deeper willingness to be honest about the contents of our hearts and to relinquish control of our desires and of our growth. It is a response to God's own invitation to deeper communion with the Holy.

As we anticipate God made flesh in Christ Jesus, we dare to relinquish control, to harness our empty life-numbing habits, and to forfeit logic and reason because God often acts outside of such boundaries. Advent is a season in which we are reminded that God invites us to listen, dwell, wait, and trust in communion with one another. No one is left to discern God's life-altering activity alone, to hold God's promises alone, or to bear the burden of divine blessings without faithful companions, whether human or angelic.

The hard work of Advent reflection and waiting is mingled with the gift of time and space to dream new dreams, to bathe in pools of hope, and to stretch the canvas of our imagination wide enough for God to paint God's own visions for our lives. Advent is a season for our imaginations to run wild as we contemplate a God who becomes human. We are given a wider glimpse of God when we allow Advent to be an invitation to dream beyond our comfort zones of what we think can happen in our lives or what God can do. In Advent we receive four weeks to dwell on what God's vision might be for us and for those whose lives we touch. Four weeks to dwell on how the courage of expanding our imagination might feed into the growing kingdom of God. Four weeks to gather our wits about us for another year; preparing our bodies, minds and spirits to receive the Christ child and take him out into the world for others to see and praise, worship and obey; the Christ with whom we dream big and imagine wildly.

PART ONE
SURPRISED AND SILENCED BY GOD

Traditionally when we think of Advent we immediately call to mind Mary, Joseph, and the angel Gabriel. But in the Gospel of Luke, Zechariah and Elizabeth are the first two people we meet in the Advent narrative. Much as John the Baptist was the forerunner to Christ, his parents Zechariah and Elizabeth seem to be the forerunners for the holy family. The angel Gabriel comes to them first to astound them with good news. Yet, Zechariah and Elizabeth teach us that receiving divine good news can be fraught with all kinds of tensions and questions. It is an understatement to say that Zechariah and Elizabeth are caught by surprise. Their shock dumbs them into silence and seclusion, affording them time to dwell with the news. The story of how Zechariah and Elizabeth come to bear their son, John, only takes up one chapter of Luke's Gospel, but it is replete with enough life and faith lessons to sustain us for weeks.

It is easy to imagine Zechariah and Elizabeth as the elderly couple we might adopt as unofficial grandparents. They were good God-fearing people recognized by their community as devout and faithful, and, according to scripture, they lived blameless lives. "Both of them were righteous before God" (Luke 1:6). Zechariah belonged to a priestly order, and Elizabeth was a descendant of Aaron, Moses' right-hand man.

An endearing couple who seemed to have lived quiet, obedi-ent lives and whom we would hope had experienced great joy and satisfaction. But from the very beginning of the Ad-vent story we are reminded that life is often unfair; and even devout, obedient people harbor the tension of unanswered prayers and bear the weight of unmet desires. "But they had no children, because Elizabeth was barren, and both were get-ting on in years" (Luke 1:7). To be a barren woman in that society meant enduring personal disgrace, and we can imag-ine that Elizabeth and Zechariah were tempted to imagine themselves cursed by God or somehow outside God's favor. How might Zechariah have felt because Elizabeth could not have children? How did this affect their marriage? Many ques-tions remain unanswered by the biblical text, but we might find countless ways to immerse ourselves in the story. Whom of us has not struggled with unanswered prayer, lived with the longing of unmet desire, feared how our community would judge us based on circumstances beyond our control, or based our self-worth on the oftentimes compassionless standards of society?

And yet for Elizabeth and Zechariah, beyond the shame also lay the fact that children secured a family's future in countless ways: to continue the bloodline, to care for aging parents, and to extend the long promised Abrahamic blessing to the world. Who would take up Zechariah's priestly duties? Having a child was steeped in significance for an Israelite cou-ple. The Advent story we associate with the joy of Christmas actually begins with deep sorrow and longing. But thankfully, in the kingdom of God there is always more to the story than meets the eye.

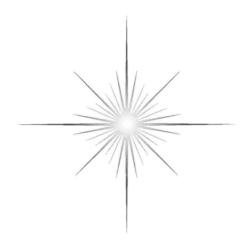

WEEK ONE

Zechariah

Luke: 1:5-19; Jeremiah 33:14-16;
Psalm 25:1-10; 1 Thessalonians 3:9-13

DAY 1

Waiting with Unanswered Prayer

Luke 1:5-11

As we begin to reflect on the story of Zechariah and Elizabeth, the first questions we might ask are, "How can Elizabeth be barren if she and Zechariah were such faithful Jews?" and "Doesn't God reward faithfulness?" There is no easy answer to these questions. And there are countless ways in which we could respond to the seeming unfairness of Zechariah and Elizabeth's situation. Many of us could probably name someone (if not ourselves) in a similar situation of having led an earnest life of faithfulness and yet living in the reality of unanswered prayers. Perhaps we are waiting patiently to meet a fitting life partner or to have that long-desired first child. Perhaps we are waiting for vocational clarity that would allow us to use our God-given gifts and passions. Perhaps we are waiting for enough financial resources to go back to school or to meet pressing needs of our family. It would be normal and expected for feelings of anger, frustration, defeat, and resignation to creep into our spirits. Such feelings are not wrong and can faithfully be acknowledged.

We are told that Zechariah prayed for Elizabeth to conceive. What the text does not share is the intensity and range of emotion that must have accompanied those times of prayer. It would be understandable if, in his disappointment, Zechariah experienced a crisis of faith, but this is not his reaction.

Zechariah was of the priestly order and had commitments to his community. He was bound to God in ways that were amplified by his years of faithful service and devotion. Instead of describing a faith crisis, the text informs us that Zechariah continues his priestly duties. He attends to his faith while bearing the reality of his unanswered prayers and God's seeming silence. In the midst of doing what is required of him in good faith, Zechariah opens himself to encounter the holy. And God shows up.

During Advent we have permission to sit with Zechariah and Elizabeth for a while before jumping too quickly into Angel Gabriel's visit. Zechariah and Elizabeth know something about longing and waiting. They must also know something about the difficulty of maintaining faith and hope. And yet, scripture only speaks of their righteousness before God. We are left wondering what it looked like for Zechariah and Elizabeth to express their yearnings, their desires, and their grief before God. We know from the witness of the Psalms that acknowledging one's desires and one's sorrows before God was part of how Israel communicated with God. So if Zechariah and Elizabeth were devout then surely their faithfulness included prayers that open their hearts to God in sincerity and vulnerability.

Prayer

God, teach us to be patient during times that make us uncomfortable. Help us open our lives to you in honesty and vulnerability. Amen.

DAY 2
Lament

Psalm 25:1-10

Psalms of lament have a certain structure to them. They include a recognized cry for help, an expression of the psalmist's circumstances, a plea for the forgiveness of past sins, an expression of trusting God, and a prayer that God will vindicate the psalmist in some way. Psalm 25 is a psalm of lament. Normally when we think about Advent we conjure up preparations for Christmas and beginning the busyness of the holiday season. We are all supposed to be of good cheer. We anticipate the birth of the Christ child and remember God's crazy love for us. But if we pay attention to the many stories within the Advent narrative, we might find that there exist necessary spaces for lamentation. A barren Elizabeth and a childless Zechariah were familiar with lament, even as they continued to pray for God's favor.

In its peculiar way lamenting is an act of faith because it speaks to our understanding that things are not as they should be. Women should not be barren. Family lines should not have to die. The elderly should always have someone to provide them with good and loving care. Zechariah and Elizabeth worshiped a God who also knew of lament. How many times did the God of Abraham, Isaac, and Jacob lament over Israel's faithlessness? Lament happens when we take relationships seriously and find ourselves disappointed by others or even by our own actions. Surely Zechariah and Elizabeth believed they had a genuine relationship with God and that God took their worship and their prayers seriously. To cry out for help, to acknowledge the disappointment and challenge of our situations is not incompatible with faithful waiting. As we wait, we express deep faith by continuing to speak out to God and one another of the things that are not as they should be.

Perhaps the more difficult part of lamenting comes in maintaining some element, no matter how small, of trusting that God is living and able, trusting in the inherent goodness of God, and recognizing that God too understands that in a broken world, things are not always as they should be. Lament in this manner is one more attempt at faithful living. I find it achingly beautiful to imagine God lamenting alongside Elizabeth in her state of barrenness. Which leads us to consider how we pray for one another and what role we can play in one another's lives when lament seems a good and necessary act of faith. In America, we live in a pain-avoidance culture that rarely sees any meaningful significance in sitting with discomfort. When something feels bad, society and corporations have conditioned us to self-medicate with media, food, or shopping. It may take discipline and practice to learn to appreciate the importance of lament for our soul's and our community's health. What could it look like to delve deeply enough into our unique, individual and communal pains so that we can faithfully write our own psalms of lament as a prayerful offering to God?

Prayer

Compassionate God, do you mourn when we mourn? Do you call us to learn to better name and lament our unique deep sorrows and communal pains? Show us how to be present to one another without glossing over pain and sorrow. Amen.

DAY 3
Intercession

Luke 1:10-13

Prayer has a power we will never be able to understand. We may never know how the prayers of others may have impacted our lives, or how our own prayers of intercession affect other people. When Zechariah enters the sanctuary, behind him is a community praying. Everyone understands the gravity and intensity of what it meant for the priest to enter God's presence. Praying for one another can be a beautiful way of acknowledging the demands, perseverance, and vulnerability that authentic faith requires of us. The words we offer on behalf of one another testify to our belief that God has indeed created us as a body and as a priesthood of believers whose actions matter to God.

Zechariah approaches the Temple supported by a community of believers. In an unavoidable way he faces his task alone, coming before God alone. But in powerful and mystery-filled ways the prayers of the people outside the temple support Zechariah. Yes, this was Zechariah's duty and the duty of the community, but we are all made dutiful to one another as siblings in the kingdom of God. A duty can also be a privilege when enacted with love. Who knows how else this believing community was dutiful to Zechariah and to Elizabeth? What else did Zechariah share with those who he knew to be people of God? Who else might have been praying

23

alongside Zechariah and Elizabeth regarding their desire for children? Sometimes when we find ourselves too burdened by the extent of our longings, too prayed out, or too exhausted with coming before God, we can look to others to bear our burdens prayerfully until we regain our own strength of spirit. A believing community shoulders hope when circumstances seem hopeless. A believing community speaks boldly into despair and longing and suggests that things do not have to remain as they are in the presence of a holy, imaginative God.

During Advent, as we wait for the fullness of God's promises in Christ Jesus, we are invited in humility and gentleness of spirit to whisper our longings to one another and to elicit a new depth of sharing with one another. Intercession is both a duty and a privilege, but we can only intercede when we learn to trust others with our unique yearnings. Naming the ache of our yearnings is indeed faithful. It opens wide the gift of receiving and embracing the prayers of others. It challenges us to new ways of loving one another as we learn to listen to the vulnerabilities of others and to graciously bear one another's burdens through prayer. May we begin to look around and discern with wisdom the people in our midst with whom we can share this Advent invitation. Who can help bear the weight of our longings, or whose longings can we help to bear, while still prayerfully hoping in the fullness of God's promises of abundant life?

Prayer

Christ, our Lord, you are our intercessor. You come before God in our place. You are the fullness of what it means to intercede for others. Help us reclaim the power and gift of intercession. Give us the faith to bring one another's burdens before you. Amen.

DAY 4

Remembered by God

Luke 1:13-17; Jeremiah 33:14-16

"'Do not be afraid, Zechariah, for your prayer has been heard'" (Luke 1:13*a*). It is difficult to put ourselves in Zechariah's shoes as he heard those words. How would we respond if God sent a personal messenger to tell us that our pleas had reached God's ears and all that we had desired was coming to pass? Do we have a big enough imagination to believe that our prayers can indeed rise up to God? These five verses from Luke 1 are packed with so much grace and divine kindness that it is hard simply as a reader not to be overwhelmed. How must Zechariah have felt? The angel informs him of God's abundant generosity. Not only has Zechariah's prayer been heard, but it will also be answered, bringing joy and gladness. The child who will be born to Elizabeth will be not only a gift to his parents but also a source of blessing to the people of Israel. Zechariah receives so much more than he asked for or could have imagined. At this point in the biblical narrative we know more than Zechariah about all that will come with the blessing of his son, John the Baptist. We can never underestimate what God will do with our prayers.

From the witness of scripture it seems that God acts in ways that speak to a bigger picture than we hold. God's gifts overflow from the recipient and into the wider community.

The communal benefit is not often immediately recognizable, but when God answers the prayers of biblical characters there is the opportunity for a host of people to be re-membered into the kingdom of God, if not now, then eventually. So what does this offer us, we who seek to be remembered by God in our own waiting? Enduring seasons of seeming silence from God on a particular concern of ours are usually unbearable. They can, among other things, tempt us to believe that God has forgotten about us. Instead we hold onto what we know to be true about God's character even if we don't currently experience that truth about God, no matter how deadening and lengthy the silence. We find our faith strengthened in persisting in the commitments and spiritual disciplines of our faith life, as did Zechariah. This might provide a more blessed option than permanently checking out spiritually. It is interesting to note that when God remembers Zechariah and sends the angel Gabriel to share the good news, Zechariah is where he should be. The angel does not approach Zechariah while he drowns his sorrows with table wine or complains to his neighbors. Rather, Gabriel reveals himself while Zechariah is doing what he is supposed to be doing. Our responsibilities and commitments do not stop while we lament, hope, pray, and wait. Who knows how God will meet us when we least expect it in the very place we are meant to be?

Prayer

God, you do not forget your children. You who are mother and father, remind us that nothing can separate us from your love and from your desire to be invested in your creation. Amen.

DAY 5
Devoted Doubt

Luke 1:18-19

How do we hold onto our belief in God's promises in the midst of doubt? At what point do our prayers become rote, tinged more with habit than with hope, based more on what we feel is required of us than in what is possible with God? Zechariah has a difficult time receiving the angel Gabriel's words because they do not fall in line with the reality of his and Elizabeth's circumstances. How can they have a child now, at the most unlikely time of their lives, in their old age? It goes against nature and hardly makes sense. We cannot fault Zechariah for hesitating to believe Gabriel's bold proclamation. Like Zechariah, how many of us would question Gabriel's words?

Maybe we do not talk enough about how taxing it can be to sustain belief even while actively engaged in the rituals of our faith. What happens to hope after season and season of unanswered prayer? Like Zechariah, we too desire to believe that our prayers make a difference and that God hears us and will eventually respond in some way or another. But desiring belief is not always enough to secure belief when hope is wearing thin. There are countless circumstances in our individual and communal lives in which we may find ourselves battling with doubt despite an active life of prayer and service. Who are the single men or women, the divorced or widowed in our communities who quietly struggle to believe that God can meet them in their loneliness or will hear and answer their prayers for companionship? If during our seasons of yearning we do receive what sound like genuine God-given words of comfort and assurance, and we may simply find them hard to believe because we have grown accustomed to dwelling in the space of unanswered prayer.

We can own our seasons of doubt and recognize that doubt is part of the human condition. Even devout persons like Zechariah experience doubt, and God still sends a messenger to him. Doubt is nothing of which to be ashamed or which causes God to turn from us. Doubt is a speed bump on the spiritual journey, and some of us have more speed bumps to cross than others. And yet, while acknowledging this condition, an invitation to resist getting comfortable with our doubts remains. Perhaps at this point we are thankfully reminded that God does not call us to journey alone. In our season of doubt it can help to remember that we have a community of persons behind us, praying, waiting to hear of our spiritual experiences, hoping to share their own stories and learning to hobble together toward deepening belief.

Prayer

Gracious God, you know us better than we know ourselves. Our doubt does not surprise you. And we know that it does not prevent you from remaining present with us and working in our lives. We give you thanks for this and pray that you help us to trust in the reality of who you are. Amen.

DAY 6
Doubt and the Believing Community

1 Thessalonians 3:9-13

It can be scary to admit to ourselves that we are experiencing doubts. We might readily and falsely assume that feelings of doubt must equate to not being good enough Christians or some other internal default that we alone encounter. We slip into periods of questioning God or teetering on the line of resignation for many reasons. No clear guidelines exist on when doubt is appropriate or inappropriate. Often we find ourselves experiencing seasons of doubt, and during those seasons, it does little good to conjure up all the possible ways we must be spiritual failures. Sometimes the most helpful thing to do is courageously share our journey with others in our faith community. Often the face of God looks strangely like people in our very midst.

Advent is a fitting time to remember that we are all members of the body of Christ. Individual efforts do not sustain faith. We need the spirit of God to assist us in all things, but we also need each other. Saint Paul was aware of this as he wrote the letter to the Thessalonian Christians so long ago. "Night and day we pray most earnestly that we may see you face to face and restore whatever is lacking in your faith" (1 Thess. 3:10). We need to learn to rely on one another in all seasons of our lives and to practice being present with those with whom we share community on a regular basis. Let us imagine a believing community that exhibits hope and belief to those who find themselves wearied by the spiritual journey. This collective bearing of strengths and struggles is one way we, as a unified body of Christ, learn to faithfully wait together for the coming fullness of God's kingdom.

How do we extend hospitality to the doubting parts of our collective body by inviting our friends and family to share openly of their faith journeys? How can God strengthen our hearts as we learn to admit our weaknesses to ourselves, to each other, and to God? We might do well to remind ourselves of periods in our lives where we truly sensed God's presence or to read through those passages of scripture that witness to God's faithfulness and steadfastness. The gift beneath all this is that God is indeed near whether we feel it or not. What a relief that God's reality and trustworthiness does not depend on our feelings. And God can be trusted with all our emotions and all our hungers, pains, fears, and doubts. The reason we are called to wait on God during Advent is because God always shows up. While we wait on God, we can lean into the believing community that trusts with us and for us. Hope and belief can be shared within the body of Christ.

Prayer

Trinitarian God, you made us in your own image. As the body of Christ we are called to strengthen, encourage, and sustain one another. As we learn to acknowledge our humanity, steep us in the grace that enables us to step into the gap of faith for one another. Amen.

DAY 7

Personal Reflection

Doubt is common to more people of faith than perhaps care to admit it. Ebbing back and forth in trust and belief is not something to be proud of but it is also not something of which to be ashamed. It is simply part of our human condition this side of heaven. Some people experience less or more of it than others. We find grace in the stories of scripture that highlight characters who experience doubt and questioning, who want proof of God's words to them. We can take spiritual refuge in people like Zechariah and the disciple Thomas who needed proof of the resurrection. Sometimes God's goodness sounds too good to be true. At times our disbelief testifies more to the expansive nature of God's grace and love than to our own human failings. And yet, the faithful challenge is not to sit in our doubts without continuing to seek glimpses of God.

When we begin to question God's presence or activity in our lives, our faith calls us to attend to the things God has entrusted us to do whether or not our prayers are answered in the way we desire. The tension of unanswered prayers is real and often quite painful. Who knows how long Zechariah and Elizabeth had been praying for a child? The endurance of their prayers stems from a discipline of faith. Zechariah and Elizabeth are devout, but they are also human. Perhaps each time they question God and God's care for them, they permit the feelings for a while; but rather than sitting in despair and doubt, they actively choose to recall who they traditionally understand God to be. The Israelites have countless stories of God's faithfulness and presence in the history of their people. These stories are essential to remember, and the Israelites are taught to share these stories again and again with one another and with their children. Zechariah and Elizabeth have it inscribed in their hearts that God remembers God's people.

Quiet Reflection

Read Psalm 40.

- For what or whom are you waiting?
- How have you brought your longing before God?
- Describe how you have perceived God's response or lack of one.
- With whom do you share your longings and spiritual frustrations?
- What new song of praise has God given you to sing as you wait?

Read Psalm 52:8-9 and Psalm 62:1-12.

- Reflect on who you truly believe God to be.

Prayerful Challenge

What stories that come out of the history of your family, church, or other spiritual and communities remind you of God's faithfulness and presence?

What would it look like for you to cultivate an expectant spirit and an untamed holy imagination capable of receiving good news when you least expect it or believe it is possible?

WEEK TWO

Elizabeth & Zechariah

Luke 1:5-7, 20-25; Matthew 24:36-44;
Isaiah 64:1-9; 1 Corinthians 1:3-9

DAY 8

Luke 1:5-7

It is a cold word, hollow-sounding, devoid of warmth, almost iron-clad in its finality: barren. Elizabeth is a barren woman. Could anything be more devastating in a culture that prides women on the fruits of their womb? Imagine her wondering what Zechariah might secretly think of her who can bear him no heir. What must God think of her? Elizabeth is known for her devoutness, yes she is barren, apparently forgotten by God? Perhaps she is as her society claimed, held in God's disfavor on some level. All her long married life, she carries this curse, this disgrace, this burden. Elizabeth is barren.

Elizabeth carries the ache of her barrenness for most of her life. She is denied the essence of what it meant to be a woman in her historical time and place. What might she have been like? How did her unmet desire affect all aspects of her life? How many of us with unmet longing can relate to her? Elizabeth's barrenness is a testimony to the embodied nature of our spiritual lives. We worship and pray with all of who we are, our at times unyielding flesh and spirits. Every time Elizabeth prayed she did so in her barren body. She prayed with that which she yearned for God to bless and touch.

Barrenness does not simply mean that a woman cannot have children. Infertility can be fraught with all kinds of unmentioned trials and varying levels of pain. And rarely is it clean. It is messy. Enduring a miscarriage is a horrifying experience of encountering life blood seeping from your body. Not to mention the emotional trauma of infertility, the self-inflicted guilt, feelings of failure, the possible onslaught of depression. Only after we acknowledge the physical reality of barrenness can we begin to consider how such pain can transfer to other forms of barrenness. Then we can adequately name other empty spaces in our lives that feel as painful as the ache of a womb that refuses to carry life, the purpose for its creation.

Prayer

Eternal Life-Giving God, barrenness is an affront to your creating spirit. Grant us strength to endure the pain that comes with barrenness. Grant us grace to acknowledge the pain that barren women endure. Help us resist the temptation to embrace shame where you call us to embrace compassion. Amen.

DAY 9
A Song from Hallowed Space

Isaiah 64:1-9

"When you did awesome deeds that we did not expect, you came down . . . " (Isa. 64:3). People have been praying for God's self-revelation for millennia. The prophet Isaiah prayed earnestly that God would reveal God's self in a mighty way, reminiscent of previous actions toward God's beloved children. The ultimate form of barrenness is being left devoid of God because no life exists without God. But we encounter other forms of barrenness. Loneliness can be a form of barrenness because we were created for companionship. All of us, single or married, were made in the image of a Triune community of love. To desire community and companionship in various forms and to lack it can be bitterly painful. We are made to offer life to one another. In a similar sense, desiring and lacking a clear sense of vocation also can be a recognized form of barrenness. Our lives are meant to glorify God, to give life back to God by using our unique attributes, gifts, and talents.

The Incarnation is, of course, the prime example of God's "coming down." But every time God brings life into spaces we imagined were dead, with nothing left to offer, we experience another moment in which God comes down to inhabit us. Our barrenness also reminds us of our dependence on God. It reminds us that "we are the clay, and [God is] our potter; we are all the work of [God's] hand" (Isa. 64:8).

So what now? How do we live in states of barrenness and still practice the devotion of Elizabeth? Amazingly, God works through many barren wombs in scripture. Sarah has Isaac. Hannah has Samuel. Ruth has Obadiah. Elizabeth has John. From the wombs the world calls cursed, forgotten, and barren, God brings forth life used to save, heal, guide, and prepare others for the kingdom. Our own lives testify to the painful fact that barrenness is not always transformed this side of heaven. Sometimes the child is not born, the loneliness persists, the ache deepens. But we have stories that dare us to remember that God is able, that God is present, and that God is yet coming. We have the witness of scripture, but we also strain our ears to listen for similar stories within our own communities. Where is God breaking in now? Who among us has an unbelievable song to sing of God's abundant provision? Who calls us to dare to hope? "When you did awesome deeds that we did not expect, you came down . . . " (Isa. 64:3).

Prayer

Redeeming God, there is always a story to tell of your goodness, a song to sing of your faithfulness, a moment to proclaim your miracles. Tune our voices and our ears to speak of and receive such testimonies where we least expect to find them. Amen.

DAY 10
Silence

Luke 1:20-23

Traditionally we read Luke 1:20-23 as God's punishment of Zechariah for his lack of faith in God's words. The angel comes to Zechariah and speaks on God's behalf. Zechariah questions the angel's seemingly ludicrous proclamation. Then the angel basically says, "Well, it's true, but since you didn't believe me you can't say another word until you see it for yourself. Now hush up and watch." Doubt did not prevent the miracle from coming to pass; it just forced Zechariah into silent retreat.

We may not be stretching the text too to consider some additional perspectives on Zechariah's muteness. On some level, yes, how dare Zechariah question the word of God? But really he was just doing what most people would have done, seeking confirmation. "Just tell me how I can be sure. I mean look at Elizabeth and me!" What if the silence God bestowed on Zechariah was not fully punishment but also an odd blessing? What if God was offering Zechariah nine months to sit with the news, to ponder God's words, and to process the stupefied awe in which he surely found himself? What if the time of formal silence was God granting Zechariah the gift of some necessary internal solitude in preparation to receive the miracle and to dwell in God's faithfulness?

Sometimes, when God offers us a word, vision, or dream that seems too good to be true, we require a lot to believe it. It is almost as though we have conditioned ourselves to have little or no expectations of divine generosity extended toward us. We reason that if we do not get our hopes up then we will not have to worry about being disappointed. We try to safeguard ourselves from the possibility of being hurt by learning not to anticipate much. We do this not only with God but also in relationships with one another. The problem with living this way is that such a posture becomes where we are most comfortable. So when a new, life-giving word comes from God, we question it and struggle to accept it. Then we begin to elicit confirmation from other people about the impossibility of God's offer. We call up a friend and say, "This is crazy, right? I'm crazy to believe this, right? I'm just setting myself up for disappointment, aren't I?"

Maybe part of Zechariah's forced silence was to protect him from himself and from trying to have such conversation with others. God said it. Now he had to sit with God's word until he could receive it.

Prayer

Lord, your compassion extends beyond what we can imagine. Where we may only see punishment and holy reprimand, help us look for a holy invitation to a deeper understanding of you. Amen.

DAY 11

Dwelling in God's Strength

1 Corinthians 1:3-9

We have all said at one point or another, "If I just knew what would happen in the future, I would be fine!" We tend to worry about the things of which we feel uncertain. For some of us it's whether or not we will ever meet the right person. Some of us wonder if we will ever find a suitable job or be able to afford a home. It is different for everyone. But for most of us, even if we did get a favorable and time-sensitive response to our pleas or requests, we would still find something to worry about, questioning, "What if it isn't true?"

To some extent, doubt, worry, and anxiety in the face of uncertainty are human nature. Zechariah has a long nine months ahead of him. Using discipline and prayer, Zechariah can cultivate non-anxious waiting. We can all attest to the difficulty of waiting. And the reality is that most of us have to wait without any message-declaring angels showing up at our doorsteps. So how do we do it? How do we cultivate a posture of faithful living with unmet desires? No easy answer exists. But there are clear steps we can take towards learning to dwell in God's strength and encouraging one another.

Inherent in the concept of liturgy is that we habituate ourselves in practices that shape our lives toward God. Every Sunday we enact a liturgy specific to our faith tradition. Each part of the liturgy reminds us of some truth about what it means to be in covenant with God. The hymns we sing, our words of confession, our offerings, our prayers, and several other liturgical aspects reveal aspects of God's covenant relationship to us as individuals and as a community. We can learn to wait faithfully and to dwell in God's strength by creating daily liturgies that shape our lives around God.

Beginning a practice of praying regularly with someone can be a helpful way to remind each other of God's goodness and steadfastness. So often we get lost in our own perspectives. As a community of believers we can encourage one another by remembering God's faithfulness in the past and God's promises for the future. Another practice we can work into our daily liturgies is the discipline of thanksgiving. Our intentional recognition of what we are grateful for shifts our minds to acknowledging our dependence on God and on one another. The God who meets our needs does not decide to stop one day. Like Zechariah, we can practice attending to the rituals of our faith and trusting God to meet us as we do the things disciples are called to do: serving, praising, praying, and more.

For those of us who sense we are waiting on a specific word from God, we do well to pray for God's help in waiting until God's word comes to pass. As we learn the challenging discipline of patient waiting, we open ourselves to being formed in richer and deeper ways that enable us to receive God's gifts more fully.

Prayer

God, help us cultivate daily liturgies of life that remind us that everything we do is an opportunity for worshiping you and being formed more and more into your likeness. Amen.

DAY 12
Divine Preparation

Luke 1:24-25

After Zechariah's visit from the angel, he returns home with nothing to say to his wife. But soon, to Elizabeth's astonishment, she becomes pregnant. Elizabeth remains in seclusion for the next five months, and it is just as well given Zechariah's muteness. What can there have been to say? Sometimes contemplation is the most fitting response to God's word or action in our lives.

In traditional religious circles, we are rarely taught the value of quiet contemplation. We are a "doing culture" by habit and conditioning. Even when we go on church retreats, we expect an agenda of speakers, workshops, and activities. Most of us would consider a silent retreat an unreasonable way to spend our time when our to-do lists seem unending. But carving out space for contemplation and solitude can invite God to speak into our lives and offer us an opportunity for us to steep in the depth of what God is already doing and saying. Elizabeth has five uninterrupted months of quiet solitude to take in the reality of her growing miracle. Not even her husband's voice can intrude on this time of reflection. Both Elizabeth and Zechariah are forced into holy retreat to dwell on what God is doing in their lives.

What thoughts go through Elizabeth's mind? Does she spend some time praising God? Does she cry out of disbelief and awe? Does she find herself praying each day out of fear that her pregnancy might end in miscarriage? Does she ask God to prepare her to care for a baby in her old age? Does she daydream of how she would eventually share her news with women in her community? The text offers nothing definitive about her five secluded months. And perhaps that is appropriate. Some things should simply remain between an individual and God.

Pondering scripture we do not see any examples of God rushing through things. Our sense of timeliness differs from God's. God's words, like a fertilized seed, need time to embed themselves in us, to take root, to be nourished in us, to grow, and then to bear fruit at God's appropriate timing. Elizabeth is not just pregnant with a child. She and Zechariah are both pregnant with a seed of trust, belief, and faith. God's word was embedding itself and taking root in both of them. And they needed time.

Prayer

God, your word takes time to bear fruit. Teach us to cultivate our bodies, minds, and spirits to be fertile ground for you. Amen.

DAY 13

Matthew 24:36-44

"Keep awake therefore, for you do not know on what day your Lord is coming" (Matt. 24:42). Spiritual retreats exist for the sake of spending time with God and discerning the present state of our spiritual lives. There are endless ways to structure retreats but one popular way is to embark on silent retreats. Rarely will God force us into silence as God did Zechariah. Neither will many of us find five months of seclusion as did Elizabeth. In our day and age with its competing commitments and responsibilities, we must be intentional about creating silent time with God. This will not be easy.

Beyond prioritizing time for silent periods with God, we may discover inner resistance to our efforts. The idea of being alone with our own thoughts and with God can be intimidating. When we have cleared our lives of distractions and pause to sit in the ensuing space, many surprising and unavoidable feelings and thoughts can surface in our minds and hearts. Furthermore we may hear not only our true selves but also what God is trying to speak into our lives. Silence forces us to name our sources of meaning, value, and identity. It creates room for our buried desires, fears, and other emotions to be heard. Once these emotions surface, we can begin the hard work of attending to them and moving toward spiritual, emotional, and mental health. It is no wonder we do not run more quickly and enthusiastically toward silent retreats or incorporating spaces of silence into our daily spiritual practices. Thankfully God knows us better than we know ourselves. God knows that our growth often requires the transformative journey through seasons of silence in which we learn to listen for God, attend to God, and begin the work of honoring our deepest selves made in God's image.

The more we inhabit silence, the better our hearing becomes. When we step back into the noise of our world, our hearing is a bit more fine-tuned and more likely to catch God's whispers. In this way, we learn to stay alert and awake. Imagine the formation that Zechariah and Elizabeth endured during their quiet season. Who knows what holy sounds they hear, what new self-discoveries they make in their old age? Who knows how God is preparing them for the events yet to come: Mary's visit; John's cousin Jesus; the way John would be raised; John leaving for the wilderness, his ministry, his imprisonment, his death. As God works in our lives now, God is also preparing us for what lies ahead. When we quiet ourselves long enough to listen for God and to God, we also join in the preparation.

Prayer

Lord, sometimes your silence is deafening. Help us navigate our way through it. Help us grow more accustomed to finding the gifts hidden in the silence and to reveal them to one another. Amen.

DAY 14
Personal Reflection

Waiting is difficult business. Sometimes the hardest work is staying still and trusting that God works even in silence. We want the confirmation of burning bushes, pillars of fire, and visiting angels. That is not the stuff of ordinary life, but it does not mean that miracles are outdated or that we cannot expect God to speak new and even unbelievable possibility into our individual and collective lives. There is something to be said for conditioning ourselves to anticipate these possibilities. Most of us do not wake up ready and able to receive or understand God's words. We have to train ourselves to become the type of earthly vessels that can endure the challenging joy of waiting on God, whether we are waiting for the Christ child or for an answer to prayer. We need ways of training ourselves in strength, patience, courage, and endurance. Spiritual disciplines like prayer, solitude, fasting, and scripture reading can be useful resources for training in daily discipleship. They open us up, hone our hearing and our spiritual vision, and make us sensitive to the leading of the Holy Spirit in our lives.

We can practice one or more of the spiritual disciplines to help guide our reflection, discernment, and action around the circumstances we bring before God and how we invite God to prepare us during our seasons of waiting. Part of that preparation might be God's invitation to us to consider our attitudes, motivations, and perspectives at this season of life. We wait in confidence and hope not because of who we are but because of whom we trust and believe God is: faithful, steadfast, full of loving-kindness, true to God's word, and present with us.

Quiet Reflection

Read Psalm 37.

- What advice does the psalmist give on what to do while waiting on God?

Read Lamentations 3:22-28.

- How does this passage encourage you during the waiting of Advent?

- What does "seeking the Lord" (Lam. 3:25) look like for you during this season?

Prayerful Challenge

Rewrite in your own words one of the passages you just read. Make it applicable to your unique situation, or compose your own short psalm on waiting because you believe in God's character.

PART TWO
PREPARATION AND LABORING
WITH GOD'S PROMISES

The psalmist pleads with God, "Make me to know your ways O Lord; teach me your paths. Lead me in your truth and teach me, for you are the God of my salvation; for you I wait all day long" (Ps. 25:4-5). In the earnestness of this prayer we get some sense of what waiting means for this psalmist. It is not a passive waiting on God but a waiting that anticipates growth, development, and guidance. Even when the waiting period is painful the psalmist can pray for openness to what God desires him to learn within this space.

When the circumstances of our lives suggest that God is calling us to a season of waiting, we rarely put all other aspects of our lives on hold. Waiting on God is not a call to quiet resignation and thumb twiddling. Rather, even as we might be called to quiet reflection, we are also invited to wait on God while pursuing our other activities and commitments. The Advent texts suggest that inherent in the waiting season is a season of preparation where we have the opportunity to sit with God's word and to pay attention to other ways in which God might be calling us to grow. Each season of our lives provides opportunities for us to discover new and continuing ways that God is speaking to us, guiding us, and teaching us.

Mary, Elizabeth, and John offer ways to imagine what preparing and laboring with God's word might look like in different circumstances. Sometimes we are called to prepare through relationships with one another. Sometimes we prepare by shedding old thoughts and practices in order to live into new ones that lead to fuller life. These possibilities take time to experience, and God's timing is different than ours. Usually we think of God's timing despairingly because we assume we know what's best for us. But the scripture passages for the third week of Advent suggest that what we perceive as slowness of action is actually God's patience with us. God graciously affords us the time we do not even acknowledge we need to prepare us for God's coming in Christ Jesus and for God's blessings all along the way.

WEEK THREE

Elizabeth, Mary, & John

Luke 1:39-45, 53, 56; Matthew 3:1-12;
James 5:7-10; Isaiah 40:1-11; Isaiah 61:1-4, 8-11;
2 Peter 3:8-15; Luke 3:1-18; Malachi 3:1-4

DAY 15

Wait and Prepare

2 Peter 3:8-15; Luke 3:1-6; Isaiah 40:1-11

Advent preparation manifests itself in how we cultivate habits of waiting "for these things" (2 Pet. 3:14)—for God's coming, for our full communion with God, and for other things unique to our circumstances. To live "without spot or blemish," (2 Pet. 3:14) is not a call to perfection this side of heaven. That is something no human, except for Christ, could ever attain. Rather, it is a call to acknowledge the spaces in our lives where God may be inviting us into abundant living but which necessitate shifts in our perspectives, attitudes, and behaviors.

John the Baptist calls us to seek repentance. In attempting to live without spot or blemish, we are called to turn from our misdirected ways of living; from the daily habits and thought patterns that tempt us to deny Christ is Lord, God is good and able, and God's word is unfailing. As we wait, we rely on God's Spirit to keep us turning ever so slightly each day toward God, shifting our crooked ways straighter, as we align ourselves with God's vision for kingdom living. Yes, this is hard work; but we cannot bypass the message of Isaiah 40. God does not expect us to set our own ways straight by our own efforts or good intentions.

"He will feed his flock like a shepherd; he will gather the lambs in his arms, and carry them in his bosom, and gently lead the mother sheep" (Isa. 40:11). The prophet paints a striking image for this season of Advent. God is fittingly portrayed as a mother caring for her young in the most intimate way, carrying them upon her breast. Such an image can greatly alter the way we see ourselves before God while we wait. We seem prone to imagine God as a stern judge or a distant surveyor. But a mothering image connotes a deity devoted to our well-being, committed to nurturing and remaining present with us. Beyond the comfort and care a mother offers, this image also invites us to think of other motherly attributes God might hold. How would it change the way we wait if we imagine a God who labors with us, bears us, delivers us, and endures us as a mother with child? When a child is under duress of any sort how much more does the mother ache alongside her offspring, even if she knows that everything will work out in the end?

Prayer

Loving God, we cannot deny the challenge of waiting on you. We cannot deny the way you love us as a mother loves her child. Remind us, as we wait on you and for you, that we are not alone in our challenges and anticipation. Amen.

DAY 16
The Refiner's Fire

Malachi 3:1-4

We worship a God whose purpose for our lives is always more expansive and pervasive than we can imagine for ourselves. There is a sense in which we are never simply waiting for what we have been promised. God's vision for us as individuals is always somehow connected to God's love for creation. As a result, we never gain full insight into what God desires for our lives and how God might bring God's desires to fruition. We can be certain of one thing: transformation into God's image and God's purpose requires that we pass through God's refining fire. Being made holy is not a one-time deal; it is an ongoing process that continues until we are fully reconciled with Christ at his second coming. During our lives we experience intense trials that we can use to refine our spirits. The key idea to remember is that we pass "through" and do not remain in the fire.

There is a noteworthy difference between the fire that refines and the one that extinguishes or consumes. Refining is the process of removing impurities from a substance to increase its value. It is an exacting effort that requires constant attention from the one refining the metals. Certain metals cannot remain in the fire too long. Every substance has its limit if the value is to be sustained. Someone not in the business of refining would have no idea of the specific details if he merely watched a metalsmith at work. But the smith knows that the metal's utmost value derives from shedding certain properties. The refining process gets to the intrinsic purity of a substance. It is a beautiful metaphor to liken God to a refiner who attends to our lives for the sake of helping us reach our authentic and most life-giving selves. During the process of refining and waiting, God watches us intently. God stays attentive and focused because the refining process necessitates such attention.

We may find it difficult to accept that we need refining, especially if everything in our lives looks perfect from the outside. In the heat of God's refining fire, the things that hinder us from experiencing abundant life in God and community melt away. We can cooperate with God during the space, time, and means of refining; or we can resist and close ourselves off to what God has in store. Inherent in our seasons of silence, reflection, and waiting is an invitation to reflect on circumstances, habits, thought patterns, or ways of being in the world that keep us from believing in God's endless possibilities and in our part in God's work of reconciling the world to God.

Prayer

God who refines and purifies, we give you thanks for your perfect timing even when we fail to understand it or to be patient. Teach us how to cooperate with your refining work in our lives. Remind us that our growth is benefits ourselves and our communities. Amen.

DAY 17

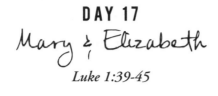
Mary & Elizabeth

Luke 1:39-45

In truly stunning fashion, God orchestrates Mary and Elizabeth's pregnancies six months apart. It is a testament to God's care and provision that each woman has someone to journey with as she navigates the peculiar seasons in which she finds herself. The gift of a believing community can make all the difference in the form our challenging waiting seasons take. By intentionally seeking out one another, Mary and Elizabeth journey together and support each other. They affirm God's miracle-working power in each of their lives. Their presence before each another serves as a daily reminder of God's faithfulness and a visual assurance of God's promises. Elizabeth is the first character in Luke's Gospel to name Jesus as personal Lord. In doing so she further confirms Mary's encounter with the angel Gabriel. In her last words to Mary, Elizabeth passionately speaks of her belief that God will do what God has promised. "'And blessed is she who believed that there would be a fulfillment of what was spoken to her by the Lord.'"

We should not be surprised at the divine consideration in having this young girl and this old woman wait together for the fulfillment of God's respective words to them. God exists within a holy community, the Trinity. God's self is a thriving community, and God created us to flourish in our interconnectedness and mutual support of one another. We need one another to remind us that all things are possible with God and to help us trust the narrative that God's reign is both at hand and still to come. In the midst of uncomfortable waiting, we need voices that also speak to our blessedness. Sharing our stories adds perspectives that can bolster our faith when life overwhelms, frightens, or takes us by surprise.

Though journeying together is rich and powerful in its ability to sustain us in faith, belief, and hope, there is something to be said about discerning whom we invite to walk alongside us. Mary and Elizabeth were fitting for each other because they truly believed in God's ability to move beyond their understanding. They shared a similar faith imagination that could hold mystery and divine possibility in the face of what the world would call impossible. Some other person might have encouraged Mary or Elizabeth to reconsider what they "think" God spoke to them, not out of malice, but simply because we all live within different expanses of holy imagination. Sometimes what we cannot believe for ourselves prevents us from believing and hoping with others. A proactive way of embracing our waiting seasons comes in seeking out the company and encouragement of those whose spiritual lives bear witness to the depth and breadth of holy imagination needed to wait on God.

Prayer

Communing God, in your wisdom and provision you invite us to journey alongside one another. Grant us wisdom and discernment to seek out and cultivate spaces of deepening holy imaginations where we can wait expectantly for you and with one another. Amen.

DAY 18
A Holy Friendship

Luke 1:56; James 5:7-10

The narrative leaves out so much information concerning the relationship between Mary and Elizabeth. Perhaps we can imaginatively consider the space they shared during Mary's three-month visit. Given their experiences, they would undoubtedly have relished the chance to ponder the holy words spoken about their miraculous pregnancies. They could share their excitement as well as their fears, possible anxieties, and insecurities of being suited for the tasks before them. Even with the level of faith they possessed, they must have experienced moments, if not days, of restlessness, worry, and anticipation. Elizabeth and Mary could strengthen one another's hearts. Perhaps they prayed together regularly. Maybe the wisdom and trials of Elizabeth's years provided comfort and security to a frightened though courageous Mary.

Advent seems as much a time to dwell in holy friendship as a time to wait on God. Ultimately, we are all called to friendship with God, and we imitate this divine call to friendship as we practice sharing ourselves and our stories with one another. In our congregations and faith communities, we laud romantic relationships and focus all our relational energies on the states of marriages or single people. Our foundation for understanding God's covenantal love for us has become steeped in romantic and sexual ways of being together. Such spaces do provide avenues for God's redeeming love, but Jesus was never married or romantically involved with anyone as far as we know. And when Christ speaks of his way of relating to his beloved disciples, he calls them his friends. Friendship is another way of being in covenant with God.

We have allowed our culture's obsession with romance and sex to dictate how we view life-giving relationships. We have dulled friendship's ability to illuminate the corners of our lives. We can endure very little without the support of friends. Choosing to open ourselves in friendship and to expose our vulnerabilities relieves the weight of carrying our burdens alone.

When God's promise not to leave us alone finds fulfillment in the people God sends to be with us. Sit quietly during this season and prayerfully reflect on the friends who remind us of who we are, who challenge us to live into who we are called to be, and who accept us at every stage of the journey. These people mirror God's love and patience in our lives. How do we mirror God's presence in the lives of those who call us friends?

Prayer

Holy God, in Christ Jesus you call us friends. Equip us to be friends who offer sustenance to one another as we learn of covenantal love from our friendship with you. Amen.

DAY 19

John the Baptist

Matthew 3:1-12

John the Baptist appears in the wilderness. How he got there is up to much speculation. Folklore has it that when King Herod ordered all the young baby boys under two years old to be killed Elizabeth took John and hid in the wilderness. Zechariah apparently was killed at the Temple because he refused to give the location of his family. Again this is all legend. We have no way of knowing what actually happens to John's parents, but we know the angel Gabriel instructs them to raise him as a Nazarene, one who vows to be set apart for God (Num. 6:1-21). From childhood John must have practiced a disciplined life, actively focused and attentive to the call of God. What sort of man is John the Baptist? He is most likely an enigmatic figure. The scriptures say he comes "neither eating or drinking," so he is not overtly social and seems to attract people merely by his presence and preaching. He doesn't perform miracles like Jesus. John's mission is to prepare the way for Jesus, and, as such, he is remembered as no other in history. Yet, even John faces challenges both during his preparing and waiting in the wilderness and in his calling to mission.

The wilderness motif is apt for Advent because the difficulty of waiting may feel like a rough wilderness. But it harbors an invitation to reflect on the wilderness motif as one in which John was prepared to be Christ's forerunner. Americans live in a culture of excess. We are conditioned to think that more is better, and extravagance is fulfilling. John offers the possibility that seasons and spaces of austerity can redirect our focus to the things of God if we choose to take advantage of such opportunities. How is John's spirituality shaped by his time in the wilderness? Does wilderness living allow him to endure the necessary sacrifices and trials of his ministry? Does his experiences of God's provision and care sustain him when life proves taxing? John must be a man of extraordinary character and integrity.

If we envision our current period of waiting on God as a sort of wilderness, what might be the strengths and graces we could cultivate to prepare for the promised season? How can we embrace waiting as an invitation to live by faith and to grow in gratitude for God's patience with us and God's perfect timing?

Prayer

Abiding Lord, you call us to prepare a way for you even as you prepare a way for us. Grant us foresight to pray for the strength, courage, and wisdom we will need in this season. Amen.

DAY 20
What Are You Waiting For?

Isaiah 61:1-4, 8-11; Luke 1:53; Luke 3:7-18

We assume the time John the Baptist spends waiting and preparing in the wilderness is in order to steep his identity in God. From before John's conception, God has claimed his life. John's primary identity will always be in relation to Jesus and in how John lived out his call to ministry. Someone like John is always bound to make people, including us, uncomfortable because his existence points us away from ourselves and toward the kingdom of God. We do not naturally and without some inner resistance make the shift from self to God. John's life and ministry compels us to consider the question, "What are we truly waiting for in this Advent and in our lives?"

Our personal longings, for which we beseech God and wait on God's answer, are valid; but we remind ourselves that God's self-revelation and promised fulfillment is always intended for healing and reconciliation in the larger community. We must ask ourselves how we can hold vigil for the groaning of humanity that is larger and more expansive than our own. How do we learn to sync up our personal stories with the Story and stay open to being subsumed by God's work in the world? This is ultimately what Elizabeth and Mary have to contend with as their children grow up. Elizabeth and Zechariah have longed for and prayed for a child their entire lives. God answered their prayers but not simply for their personal satisfaction. John was indeed a source of deep joy for his parents as the angel Gabriel had pronounced (Luke 1:14). Yet we do not remember John primarily as the blessed answer to prayer or the miracle child of Elizabeth and Zechariah; we remember him as the one who came to prepare the way for the Son of God. Elizabeth's hunger was only satisfied in God's ensuing plan to satisfy the deep hunger of the world.

So where does this leave us? How might we think about the things for which we personally long and wait? What does God's desire for a reconciled and healed world have to do with our desire for children, companionship, vocational fulfillment, and other yearnings? This question has no easy or definitive answer. There is nothing wrong with having our particular deep desires and prayerfully laying them before God. We were created to flourish in the gift of God's world while waiting for the fullness of the kingdom. Yet we remain open to having our desires trumped by what God may invite us into for the sake of fostering God's kingdom on earth as it is in heaven.

Elizabeth and Zechariah bear witness to how our deep desires can match up with God's desires for us. But God's longings for us always seem connected to a bigger picture that includes others. From what we see in scripture, God's story always makes room for those whom society wants to push to the margins for all sorts of reasons. Part of waiting in Advent involves wrestling with the tensions we discover as we let God's desires speak into ours.

Prayer

Lord, make us willing to hold and nurture the desires you plant within us. Amen.

DAY 21

Personal Reflection

When God calls us, God equips us with holy strength and human support. No one bears God's word alone, and yet, nothing can make us available to God but the state of our hearts and spirits. The refiner's fire can have many manifestations. It is a call to repentance, introspection, and communal engagement. During Advent there is a need to be called apart from and called into a journey with the community of God.

No amount or configuration of words can do justice to the experience of the Annunciation. How does one describe the descent of a message-laden angel to the home of a seemingly average teenage girl to tell her that the Spirit of God will soon inhabit her youthful womb and she will give birth to the Son of God? There are not enough words in any language to capture that event. And yet what we have in scripture affords us some idea of what God is like and what faithful servanthood resembles.

In chapter one of Luke's Gospel, we learn that God is not bound by our expectations or limitations. God presumably believes that we are more capable than we think to endure certain experiences and to assist God in divine work in the world. God also anticipates our needs in fulfilling God's desires for us. The fact that Mary found favor with God indicates a previously existing awareness and attention to Mary before Gabriel's visit. This is a good reminder when we are tempted to think God has forgotten us. God is always aware of us. God embraces our questions and is capable of responding to us regardless of what we think of God's response.

We see varied aspects of the faith journey played out through the responses of the Advent characters. Zechariah's questioning of Gabriel hints at our normal tendency to doubt what sounds too good to be true and what is beyond our capacity to imagine. Elizabeth's seclusion and John's sojourn in the wilderness suggests the wisdom of acknowledging that certain seasons do call us to time apart with God. In the Annunciation narrative, Mary's quiet courage, boldness of spirit, and obedience to God speak greatly of her devotion to God.

Quiet Reflection

Read Luke 1:26-45.

• How might Mary's reaction to Gabriel's surprising visit have been different?

• What other emotions might we have expected from someone in Mary's situation?

Read Zephaniah 3:14-20.

• Meditate on verses 19-20.

• Think outside of your immediate community and consider to what group of people today could this passage be good news?

Prayerful Challenge

Spend some intentional time in prayer over the next week asking God to open your eyes to someone whom you might normally pass over. Reflect on why you have not paid attention to this particular person before. Ask God if there is anything for you to learn about what it means to be a part of God's family from this new awareness.

PART THREE
TRUSTING AND RECEIVING GOD'S WORD

Trusting God is a daily discipline that cannot be dependent on how we feel. There will be countless times when we do not feel like trusting because circumstances seem insurmountable. Yet, we will ourselves to claim the truth of God's trustworthiness because we claim the truth of God's unchanging character. Scripture and community are indispensable to our waiting seasons. Scripture holds countless testimonies of God's enduring faithfulness throughout the history of God's people. It holds countless stories of people just like us who received God's word and struggled to trust God's word and often tried to take matters into their own hands when God seemed to be moving too slowly. Meditating on these stories exercises our faith muscles and reminds us that waiting on God is common to the human condition.

The power of a believing community can do wonders in how we wait in hope. A community helps us discern how God calls us and speaks into our lives, keeping us accountable to spiritual integrity and affirming or challenging our discernment as necessary. It is important to have people with whom we can prayerfully share our spiritual journeys and who can help us name the new realities that God might be birthing in our lives. A community can support us as we name these new realities and learn to live into our expanding or changing sense of identity as flourishing children of God.

Part of receiving God's word comes in learning to offer thanksgiving even as we anticipate the fullness of things to come. Expressing our gratitude is an act of asserting our belief that God is true to God's word. It is also a means of cultivating the type of spirit that recognizes the fitting response to God's act of love. As we move into the fourth week of Advent, we can be thankful for much. During this week, we transition from waiting to celebrating Jesus' birth and the season of Christmas.

God is indeed faithful to God's promises. The risk of expectant waiting is proven beautifully worthwhile.

WEEK FOUR

The Community Trusts the Word

Luke 1:39-80; Isaiah 7:10-16; Psalm 80:1-7; John 1:1-14
Romans 1:1-7; Matthew 1:18-25; Psalm 89:1-4;
Psalm 126; Zephaniah 3:14-20; Psalm 146:5-10

DAY 22
Seeing Those Who Dream

Psalm 126; Zephaniah 3:14-20; Psalm 146:5-10

In the whirlwind of holiday activity, we can easily forget that the characters of the Advent and Christmas narratives were nothing like us. Zechariah, Elizabeth, Mary, John, and, yes, even Jesus were Middle Eastern people of a lower socioeconomic class than most of us reading this book. Furthermore, as an ethnic and religious people they were marginalized from the mainstream Roman culture and looked upon disdainfully by government and high church officials. The Jewish people were rooted in a history of oppression and they were awaiting a messiah who would usher in a new heaven and earth by rescuing them from the varied forms of systematic injustice they endured.

"When the Lord restored the fortunes of Zion, we were like those who dream" (Ps. 126:1). Would we think of Advent in a different way if we tried to imagine the promise and hope of Advent from the perspective of someone from a different socioeconomic, cultural, or racial background than our own? How might a congregation of migrant farm workers live and pray during the season of Advent? How might a group of Christian inmates at a federal prison pray during the season of Advent? How might the people who live in neighborhoods we try to avoid pray during the season of Advent? These are worthy considerations.

Many of us can relate to the strange phenomenon of how two siblings from the same family can be so drastically different from each another. But because we are family, we find ways to both embrace and celebrate our differences. Many of us were also raised understanding and believing that if a family member has a need, then we do what we can to be present out of love and familial responsibility. Few of us would ignore the plight of a brother or a sister.

In the family of God, our responsibility to each other extends beyond race, ethnicity, socioeconomic background, and sexual orientation. When persons are in need, we all bear a familial responsibility to be present. It might take us some time to discern to whom and how God invites us to be present with our unique gifts and circumstances. Where there is economic poverty, we are called to recognize our siblings among the poor. Where there is social and political injustice, we are called to recognize our siblings among those who bear the brunt of injustice.

As God is often made manifest to us through the people we encounter, we need not be surprised if part of the invitation of waiting in Advent involves inquiring of God how we might be channels of love and even answers to the prayers of those who wait for restoration of body, mind, and spirit.

Prayer

Lord, help us see your reflection in those whom we most readily assume are different from us. Help us learn to be part of the answers to one another's prayers. Amen.

DAY 23

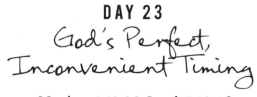
God's Perfect, Inconvenient Timing

Matthew 1:18-25; Isaiah 7:10-16

If anyone knows about God's inconvenient timing, it is Mary and Joseph. If they are already engaged, why can't God just wait a few months and then visit Mary? Or why can't God show up when Joseph was also present? Why make matters more difficult than they need to be? We can suggest many reasons, but a particular one could be that God wants there to be no doubt that God is behind Mary's pregnancy. There is no room for error. Plus, who knows how Joseph might receive Gabriel, or why Mary needs that intimate moment alone with God's messenger? Certainly because of the way it happens, Mary is called to even more trust and dependence on God. God has to make this event clear to Joseph. God has to ensure that Mary is provided for. And Mary says yes to God without having any idea how these other concerns will be met. Mary trusts enough to believe that even if the timing is inconvenient for her, it is perfect for God.

Openness to God demands our growing acceptance that we cannot create blueprints for our own lives. Though God's character is unchanging, the ways of God are unpredictable, and there is a difference between arbitrariness and unpredictability. The former connotes a degree of randomness and lack of order. God's unpredictability never stems from a lack of order; we simply are not privy to God's order. What may seem random to us could fall right in line with God's design for our circumstances. This is a tricky idea around which to wrap our minds. We must avoid considering every circumstance we do not understand as falling within God's design. God's order never goes against God's character. The one who created us always wills the flourishing of our body, mind, and spirit. Yet, God has chosen to work within the bounds of Creation's fallen state. Life's arbitrariness and God's unpredictability are not one and the same.

This is why spiritual discernment and faith within community is a necessary element of perceiving and receiving holy disruptions—the movements of God that interrupt our life plans but ultimately bring order to our lives. Part of discernment is listening for the invitations, both the unexpected and those that come from existing circumstances and relationships. Embracing God's invitations and disruptions will often, if not always, require our courage and trust. Fear and uncertainty do not occur only in the face of perceived danger. These feelings can also arise in the face of invitations that might call us to step out of our comfort zones. Interestingly, the human spirit and mind can actively resist what is ultimately meant to be blessing.

Prayer

Lord, if only we understood your timing, our lives might appear easier. But the reality is that your timing is always perfect and fitting because you see the bigger picture of our lives. Help us learn to set our lives to your time. Amen.

DAY 24
Bearing the Word
John 1:1-14

It comes to pass. The Word of God is delivered to the world. The promise God offers, the promise Mary carries, the light that dispels darkness is born in Jesus Christ. We will never be able to understand fully the implications of the incarnate Christ. Elements of unsolvable mystery will always surround what it means for God to become human. Though we cannot fully grasp the miracle of Jesus' birth, we can be eternally affirmed in the steadfastness and faithfulness of God.

Jesus' birth changes everything. Not only are holy promises fulfilled, but all of our futures are now subject to new beginnings and new endings. Life is most fully lived within the light that Jesus brings into the world. What can that mean for us from this day forward? We have journeyed with Zechariah through doubt and silence. We have journeyed with Elizabeth through barrenness and wonder. We have journeyed with Mary through blind faith and acceptance. How can we now journey with Christ in the midst of our assorted longings, misgivings, and worries? Jesus' birth invites us to lay down our concerns for a moment and kneel with awe and thanksgiving at the faithfulness and love of God. The longer we gaze upon Jesus, the more we realize that life as we know it can no longer remain the same. The wait for Zechariah, Elizabeth, and Mary is over, but their trust in God is just beginning.

Part of the wonder of this season is that God chooses to bring about the mystery of Jesus' birth with human help. We see God's work woven into the intercession of Zechariah, the courage of Elizabeth, the obedience and faith of Mary, the humility of Joseph, and the discipline and devotion of John the Baptist. Through Jesus, the Word of God, all things come into being, but we still have a role to play in the fulfillment of God's promises to an aching world. Like Zechariah, Elizabeth, and Mary, we have to listen for God's invitations into this ongoing holy drama. Our adoration of the Christ child must lead to obedience and devotion. Only then can we open our lives to God's continual life-giving disruptions.

Prayer

Holy infant, Savior, Eternal Word of God, may our adoration and praise converge in obedience and devotion. May we find our lives bound up in you. May we have the courage and the wisdom to drop our burdens long enough to bear you in our arms. Amen.

DAY 25
God Delivers on God's Word

Psalm 89:1-4; Psalm 80:1-7; Luke 1:57-66

Since God's covenant to Abram, the Jewish people have known the importance of keeping God's words on their lips. Reciting God's words aloud to their children is a way of remembering that they belong to God, who desires their total commitment and trust. Zechariah, Elizabeth, Mary, John, and all the other faithful Jews we find in the New Testament narratives are well versed in their Hebrew Bible. They know the history of God's steadfast faithfulness to God's children. They know the stories of God's commitment even when their ancestors rebelled against God. The Advent characters we meet have a clear sense of who God is and had been throughout their people's history. Both Zechariah and Mary sing aloud the fulfillment of God's words through John's birth and Mary's pregnancy. They know of God's promises because their ancestors faithfully proclaimed God's goodness throughout the generations.

It is a good practice to read the biblical passages that tell of God's loving-kindness, God's steadfastness, and God's covenant with creation. We can hold our experiences up to the testimony of scripture to see if what we believe of God falls in line with God's character throughout time. In the face of life's trials, the one constant is the unchanging character of God.

It is also fitting to recount God's faithfulness in our own lives because it reminds us of God's presence with us. God promised never to leave or forsake us. When we speak of God's goodness, we reorient ourselves to the tenets of kingdom living. God creates; we worship and praise. God initiates; we respond in prayer and commitment. God promises; we wait and trust. God calls; we answer. God dwells in us and among us; we mirror God back to each other.

Waiting for God to deliver on God's word is not easy by any means. As we wait, we may question the belief that God has given us a word upon which to wait. Our faith dances back and forth, and we need a believing community to remind us that God is trustworthy. All we can do to determine the accuracy of our hearing is wait and see what comes to pass. Faith, hope, and trust can be contagious within a faith community.

Prayer

Trustworthy God, there is no one on whom we can depend more than you. Your promises never fail. Your mercies are new every morning. Forgive us when we waver in faith. Help us to remember your history of loving-kindness that culminates in the Incarnation. Amen.

DAY 26

The Art of Faithful Naming

Luke 1:59-66; Romans 1:1-7

It is fascinating to think about how the trends of baby names in our American culture can be heavily influenced by popular movies, songs, or celebrities. We also tend to name our children after other family members or if we like the way the name sounds. In various non-Western cultures around the world, naming a child is sacred ritual given much consideration and often bestowed upon the community elders. Names in such cultures are believed to have a guiding force in a child's life as she grows to maturity. In selecting names people consider the characteristics they hope for the child, the protection they wish upon the child, or a recognition of where the child came from and to whom the child ultimately belongs.

In the Advent story, names are significant because they point to a child's divine call. Zechariah, Elizabeth, and Mary were given the task of naming their children according to God's intentions for them. John means "God is gracious/ merciful," and Emmanuel means "God with us." We might be tempted to think that being so intentional and reflective about what we name our children is taking it all too seriously. There is indeed nothing wrong with naming children after other people or because one simply likes how a name sounds. But there is value in thinking about the power that names can have in our lives, whether it is our birth names, or the names people assign us later in life, or the names we claim for ourselves. A name is an identifier. It is how we recognize who we are and who others are. Even the childish act of nicknaming can have positive or negative effects on someone. The names we bear or endure can hint at both beautiful truth and debilitating falsehoods.

Our birth names notwithstanding, the events in the Advent story invite us to ponder the art of faithful naming and what it has to do with living as though we believe in God's kingdom here on earth and as it will be in heaven. What unconscious names do we have for God, and what do they tell us about who we believe God to be and how we understand our relationship with God? In what ways do we believe God has named us, and how does this point to our place in the community of God? How do we name one another by our actions and by whom we choose to attend to or to ignore? How do we name one another in ways that speak to God's presence and that affirm our worth before God? Names matter, and they form us in ways of which we are rarely aware. This Advent, as we wait for God and on God, let us also wait to hear what new names God is calling us to live into. Let us take the time to affirm the blessedness of others by how we name them in good faith.

Prayer

Almighty God, Comforter, Redeemer, Savior, Creator, and Deliverer, remind us that your names exhaust our imagination because you are all things that offer life and love. Amen.

DAY 27

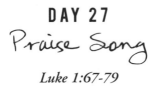

Luke 1:67-79

John the Baptist is born. Christ is born. As we reflect on Zechariah's journey, the person with whom we started this Advent season, we rejoice as he rejoices at the faithfulness of God's promises. The season of silence is over, and Zechariah can speak. The holy retreating is over. Like Zechariah, we can proclaim God's faithfulness from generation to generation. The Benedictus, the song of Zechariah that praises God and sings of freedom, is conceived out of Zechariah's nine-month silence. It is a beautiful way to embrace his powers of speech. What words can give credence to all that Zechariah has seen in the last nine months? The angel in the Temple, his aged wife pregnant, his virgin niece pregnant, his unborn son jumping at the sound of the pregnant virgin's voice, and his wife choosing to name their son John before he, Zechariah, could even speak a word. There is no better response than to begin by praising God and speaking blessing and assurance into his son's life. Unto us the Christ child is born—an even greater wonder than the birth of John. The salvation of the world is at hand. It is the season to receive God's wonderful gift and to proclaim it to the world.

God remains true to God's word to redeem us from ourselves and to provide a way to reconcile ourselves fully to God in mercy, grace, and patient love. Jesus' birth will nurture the seeds of hope God has planted within each of us and make a way where there seems to be no way. Jesus comforts those who mourn, heals those who ache, feeds those who hunger, embraces those who are lonely, and creates new life in the dead spaces within us.

As we celebrate this Christmas season, what new thoughts and habits are we cultivating? What song is building in our hearts that will speak of God's faithfulness and our freedom in Christ? To whom will we offer a word of assurance? Who in our community will embrace their identity in Christ? Who will help us embrace our own identity? What communal story will our Benedictus deliver that invites others to join in the praise of God?

Prayer

O God, Christ is born. We celebrate this gift. You are continually redeeming us and reconciling us to you. Fill our mouths with praise and thanksgiving. "By the tender mercy of our God, the dawn from on high will break upon us, to give light to those who sit in darkness and in the shadow of death, to guide our feet into the way of peace." Amen.

DAY 28
Personal Reflection

We have journeyed with Zechariah, Elizabeth, Mary, and John for the last four weeks. Jesus has come and is yet to come. The waiting of Advent is over, but we still wait for other things in our lives. We know we are not alone in our waiting, in our quiet longings, and in our occasional doubt. God is with us. Emmanuel. Our community of faith is with us, and we are present for one another. We open ourselves to the possibility of miraculous new life sprouting from what seems barren and lifeless. God is a God of all things. God is a redeeming God, a life-giving and sustaining God. We listen for the wisdom and witness from those who have gone before us and who tell of God's goodness, faithfulness, and steadfast love. We trust in the character of God when our faith wavers. We visit with one another and bear with one another. We hold silent vigils as we wait and prepare to give breath to the lyrics of praise and exultation welling up inside us. We silently and faithfully compose our own Benedictus, and we ready ourselves for Christ to come again.

Quiet Reflection

Take some time to reflect prayerfully on what this Advent season has been like for you.

- What questions in your own life have stayed with you over the course of Advent?

- What new insights have you gained?
- Who surprised you by journeying with you this season?
- What have you perceived about the significance of friendship for a flourishing faith life?

Guide for Small Groups

This resource can be shared by two friends, a small group, or even a Sunday school class who desire to move through the season of Advent together. The basic pattern for facilitating a group conversation each week can be found below. A group's facilitator will not need to spend more than thirty additional minutes beyond the preparation time of all group participants. That individual will need to prepare the group through the session by using the Quiet Reflections and Prayerful Challenges from each week. Facilitation for a group can be shared by different members of the group.

For the Facilitator

Be sure that all participants know where, when, and how long the group will meet so they feel fully prepared and informed. Each participant will need a copy of *Silence and Other Surprising Invitations of Advent*, preferably at least one full week in advance of the first session. Also it is helpful to remind group participants to bring a Bible and, if desired, a journal.

Select a setting for the gathering that is conducive to conversation. It could be a classroom, living room, or other comfortable setting. Set up the space so people will be able to see and hear one another easily. Lighting Advent candles would be appropriate for the beginning of each session as a time of quieting and prayer and to underscore the ongoing nature of the season. Advent candles can be purchased in Christian book and supply stores in your community, online at www. cokesbury.com, or from other denominational outlets.

Schedule for the four Advent gatherings to conclude as close to Christmas as possible for your group. It does not matter which day of the week you choose; any day will do.

Preparation for facilitating a group or class conversation involves two basic steps:

- Read through all of the materials for the week, taking part in the Quiet Reflections and Prayerful Challenges just as all participants will do.

- Choose which Reflections and/or Challenges to use in your gathering based on the length of time your class or group will meet.

Materials Needed
Copies of *Silence and Other Surprising Invitations of Advent* for all participants; candle or Advent candles; chalkboard, dry-erase board, or flip chart; Bible.

Guiding the Group
At the first gathering welcome everyone and ask individuals to introduce themselves if participants do not know one another.

Take a few minutes to set the tone for these gatherings and conversations by summarizing these understandings or ground rules for your time together:

- Everyone will arrive on time, and the session will end on time.
- These gatherings constitute a safe place where confidentiality will be honored.
- We will give each other room to speak and practice listening without needing to analyze, clarify, or respond.
- No one needs to feel compelled to speak or share. We will honor the presence and practice of silence.
- We will arrange for breaks as needed.

Once all have arrived, invite people to settle into the space and to enter into a few minutes of quiet. If you use Advent candles, light them at this point. (Two to five minutes)

Now invite conversation around one or all of the scripture readings for the week. Do not hurry this response time. It is, in its own way, a call to worship for the gathering. (Ten to twenty minutes)

Invite the group to share reactions and responses to the week's meditations, using the questions from the end of each week to guide the conversation. You can be very flexible in the time allotted to this segment of the group session. (Fifteen to sixty minutes)

If your group is meeting for an hour or less you could simply ask which passages or reflections caught their attention in particular ways.

If your group has a longer session together, you could read the scripture from the Quiet Reflection aloud and the whole group could work through the reflection questions together.

Advent Wreath Candlelighting Meditations

The following short meditations can be used with the weekly lighting of candles of an Advent wreath on the four Sundays of Advent and Christmas Eve. Feel free to adapt the meditations for use in Sunday school, worship, or the home. The meditations consist of a scripture reading taken from lectionary passages, as well as short prayers and one stanza of a related hymn or song from *Worship & Song*, *The Faith We Sing*, and *The United Methodist Hymnal*. The scripture readings have been divided into individual verses with the hope that all members of the group will participate in the reading. Likewise, the prayers have been divided into individual sentences. If you do not have an Advent wreath, you may use candles alone—four of similar size and color for the four Sundays (purple or blue is traditional), and a white candle in the center for Christmas Eve.

First Sunday of Advent

But in those days, after that suffering, the sun will be darkened, and the moon will not give its light, and the stars will be falling from heaven, and the powers in the heavens will be shaken.

Then they will see the Son of Man coming in clouds with great power and glory. But about that day or hour no one knows, neither the angels in heaven, nor the Son, but only the Father.

Keep alert, for you do not know when the time will come . . . in the evening, or at midnight, or at dawn. Keep awake.
                                        —Mark 13:24-26, 32, 33, 35, 37

Amazing things happen in the sky to herald the return of the Son of Man:

- Jesus, coming in the clouds,

- the sun growing dark,

- the moon failing to shine,

- and stars falling from the heavens.

So different from that first coming more than two thousand years ago:

- with angels singing of God's glory and peace on earth,

- with the single star guiding the way to the manger,

- with shepherds and wise ones—rich and poor—coming to worship.

So we watch, and wait, and stay alert, waiting again for the coming of Jesus.

And we light a single candle in preparation for that glorious day.

[Light the first candle on the Advent wreath.]

Even if the sun should grow dark,

even if the moon refuses to shine,

even if the stars should fall from the sky,

. . . we will have Jesus, the Light of the World, to shine brightly in our hearts, lighting our way.

ALL: **COME, LORD JESUS. AMEN.**

Song Recommendations

"Until Jesus Comes"

"Shine, Jesus, Shine"

"My Lord, What a Morning"

Second Sunday of Advent

[Light the first candle on the Advent wreath.]

The prophet Isaiah wrote, "See, I am sending my messenger ahead of you, who will prepare your way; the voice of one crying out in the wilderness: 'Prepare the way of the Lord, make his paths straight.'" (Mark 1:2-3)

And John, the messenger of God, proclaimed to all the people who came to him in the wilderness that they must repent of their sins and be baptized. Many people heard his message, repented, and were baptized in the river Jordan.

It has become our custom to prepare for the birth of the Messiah by decorating our cities and homes, hanging the lights inside and out, singing "Frosty the Snowman" and "Rudolph the Red-Nosed Reindeer," and measuring the quality of our Christmas morning by the number of gifts we receive.

[Light the second candle.]

As we light this second candle in preparation for the coming of the Messiah, perhaps we need to listen again to John the Baptizer's message, preparing the way of the Lord:

- make straight the paths,

- repent of your sins,

- be baptized,

- and live holy lives devoted to God.

ALL: **COME, LORD JESUS. AMEN.**

Song Recommendations
"Down by the Jordan"
"Cry of My Heart"
"Prepare the Way of the Lord"

Third Sunday of Advent

[Light the first and second candles of the Advent wreath.]

If Jesus comes to us again at Christmas this year, and if Jesus dwells within each of us, shouldn't that make a difference in who we are and how we live our lives? Hear these words from First Thessalonians:

"Rejoice always, pray without ceasing, give thanks in all circumstances; for this is the will of God in Christ Jesus for you.

Do not quench the Spirit. Do not despise the words of the prophets, but test everything; hold fast to what is good; abstain from every form of evil.

May the God of peace himself sanctify you entirely; and may your spirit and soul and body be kept sound and blameless at the coming of our Lord Jesus Christ.

The one who calls you is faithful, and he will do this."
—1 Thessalonians 5:16-24

If we seek Jesus, who is born in the manger, shouldn't we

- be at peace among ourselves?

- help the weak and the poor?

- not repay evil for evil, but always do good to one another?

- in all circumstances, give thanks?

[*Light the third candle of the Advent wreath.*]

As we light this third candle, let us remember that this is the will of God in Christ Jesus, who comes to us.

ALL: **COME, LORD JESUS. AMEN.**

Song Recommendations
"View the Present through the Promise"
"Give Thanks"
"Lift Up Your Heads, Ye Mighty Gates"

Fourth Sunday of Advent

[*Light the first three candles of the Advent wreath.*]

After the angel came to Mary and told her that she would conceive the child in her womb and would call him Jesus, Mary said, "Here am I, the servant of the Lord; let it be with me according to your word." (Luke 1:38)

And Mary sings her song of praise:

"My soul magnifies the Lord…he has scattered the proud

He has brought down the powerful from their thrones

He has lifted up the lowly

He has filled the hungry

He has provided for the poor."

—Luke 1:46-55

We marvel at Mary, the mother of the Messiah, herself a single, teenaged mother, herself poor and powerless. But she understood that the baby she would call Jesus was sent, not just to her, but to the world. He was sent

- to the hungry,

- to the weak,

- to the very young and the very old,

- to those who suffer or are in pain.

[Light the fourth candle of the Advent wreath.]

We light this fourth candle to remember Mary, the mother of Jesus. May the light of this candle also remind us that the light of Jesus shines for everyone.

ALL: **COME, LORD JESUS. AMEN.**

Song Recommendations
"Come, Let Us Dream"
"Star Child"
"Sing of Mary, Pure and Lowly"

Christmas Eve

[NOTE: On this night the lighting of the four Advent candles takes place just prior to the reading of the Gospel lesson.]

In those days a decree went out from Emperor Augustus that all the world should be registered. This was the first registration and was taken while Quirinius was governor of Syria. All went to their own towns to be registered.

Joseph also went from the town of Nazareth in Galilee to Judea, to the city of David called Bethlehem, because he was descended from the house and family of David. He went to be registered with Mary, to whom he was engaged and who was expecting a child. And she gave birth to her firstborn son and wrapped him in bands of cloth, and laid him in a manger, because there was no place for them in the inn.

[Light the Christ candle.]

In that region there were shepherds living in the fields, keeping watch over their flock by night. Then an angel of the Lord stood before them, and the glory of the Lord shone around them, and they were terrified. But the angel said to them, "Do not be afraid; for see—I am bringing you good news of great joy for all the people: to you is born this day in the city of David a Savior, who is the Messiah, the Lord. This will be a sign for you: you will find a child wrapped in bands of cloth and lying in a manger."

And suddenly there was with the angel a multitude of the heavenly host, praising God and saying: "Glory to God in the highest heaven, and on earth peace among those whom he favors."

When the angels had left them and gone into heaven, the shepherds said to one another, "Let us go now to Bethlehem and see this thing that has taken place, which the Lord has made known to us." So they went with haste and found Mary and Joseph, and the child lying in the manger. When they saw this, they made known what had been told them about this child; and all who heard it were amazed at what the shepherds told them. But Mary treasured all these words and pondered them in her heart. The shepherds returned, glorifying and praising God for all they had heard and seen, as it had been told them.

—Luke 2:1-20

ALL: **COME, LORD JESUS. AMEN.**

Song Recommendations

"Still, Still, Still"

"Thou Didst Leave Thy Throne"

"What Child Is This"

About the Author

The former Director for the Center for Theological Writing at Duke University Divinity School, Enuma Okoro received her MDiv degree from Duke in 2003. She is author of the 2010 publicly acclaimed spiritual memoir *The Reluctant Pilgrim* (Fresh Air Books, 2010) and co-author with Shane Claiborne and Jonathan Wilson-Hartgrove of *Common Prayer: A Liturgy for Ordinary Radicals* (Zondervan, 2010). Okoro is one of several poets featured in the book *At the Still Point* (Paraclete, 2010), and is a contributing writer for *Christianity Today*, *Sojourners*, ABC's *Good Morning America*, and Patheos.

Having lived on four different continents Enuma is learning to call Durham, North Carolina, home, where she juggles writing, teaching, speaking, and spiritual directing.

Visit www.enumaokoro.com
Follow on Twitter: @Tweetenuma